structures for success!

Laurie Kagan &
Dr. Spencer Kagan

Kagan

v4 ajc

Table of Contents

structures for success!

Welcome,

The following are some tips which can make the workshop more worthwhile.

★ **Meet other people.** This is an excellent opportunity to expand your network of contacts. During breaks sit next to someone you don't know, even if you've come with a group. Mingle during the breaks. Exchange ideas. Every participant has a specific area of expertise; find out what it is instead of chatting about the weather. Remember your goal sheet. Why not make it a personal goal to meet at least one person you intend to meet with or talk with on a regular basis following the workshop?

★ **Participate!** Make contributions. Actively participate in the exercises. Consider the meeting room to be a "mental gymnasium" where it's okay to run, fall and get up again. You'll benefit much more by participating in the game than sitting on the sidelines.

★ **Take notes.** Why let even one good idea get away? Taking notes will help you concentrate and organize your thoughts. Plus, they'll allow you to take a "refresher" any time in the future. Hint: make them clear as you write them. Few people ever have the luxury of rewriting their notes, no matter how good their intentions.

★ **Relate what you learn to your self.** Don't settle for "abstract" knowledge. Have your current problems, conflicts and interests foremost in your mind. As you learn new approaches and techniques, relate them to your own situation.

★ **Find "the big idea."** Occasionally push back from the details and sum it all up. Try to identify at least one "big idea" that alone will make this workshop worthwhile.

★ **Make a commitment to review your notes.** During the workshop set some time aside in the evenings to review your notes. Take out your calendar and make a one hour appointment with yourself for a month from now to "retake" the workshop. Don't put your good ideas away with your notes.

★ **Share your ideas with fellow teachers and your principal.** Share your "major learnings" with someone who can support you. We all need a support person.

★ **Enjoy yourself. Relax.** Forget about what's happening at your home or school. This is your workshop. Allow yourself to be here fully. Be yourself. Enjoy.

Sincerely,

Spencer Kagan and Laurie Kagan
Directors, Kagan Publishing & Professional Development

About Kagan

Kagan Publishing and Professional Development has its roots in a research program begun by Dr. Spencer Kagan in 1968. Dr. Kagan discovered that, worldwide, children of all ages responded with enhanced cooperativeness when placed in certain types of situations. Dr. Kagan began a research program to apply those findings to classrooms, creating simple ways teachers could structure the interaction of students. Kagan's structures not only led to greater cooperativeness, but led also to greater academic achievement, improved ethnic relations, enhanced self-esteem, harmonious classroom climate, and a range of social skills. Thus, Dr. Kagan fathered the structural approach to cooperative learning which is now used in classrooms at all grade levels, worldwide, to produce revolutionary positive results.

Dr. Kagan and his team have developed and perfected well over 150 of these simple teaching techniques or structures, such as Numbered Heads Together, Timed-Pair-Share, Pairs Compare, Kinesthetic Symbols, and Lyrical Lessons. Dr. Kagan's book, *Cooperative Learning*, is the single most comprehensive and popular book in the field having sold over a quarter of a million copies. Instead of emphasizing complex cooperative learning lessons, theme units, projects, and centers, the structural approach makes cooperative learning part of any lesson by inclusion of cooperative structures — it is an integrated approach to cooperative learning.

Because the Kagan Structures are so easy to learn and apply, Kagan participants spontaneously created the Kagan motto: **Learn it Today; Use it Tomorrow; Apply it for a Lifetime!**

Recently, the educational community has attempted to implement the theory of Multiple Intelligences. In approaching Multiple Intelligences, the Kagans have applied the same structural approach which has been so successful with cooperative learning. The Kagan Multiple Intelligences Structures have been enormously empowering to teachers worldwide. Together with Miguel Kagan, Dr. Spencer Kagan completed the most comprehensive book to date on Multiple Intelligences for teachers. In *Multiple Intelligences*, the Kagans demonstrate the power of simple MI structures which are now doing for Multiple Intelligences what the Kagan Cooperative Learning Structures did for cooperative learning. Instead of emphasizing complex Multiple Intelligences lessons, theme units, projects, and centers, the Kagan approach makes Multiple Intelligences part of any lesson by inclusion of simple

MI structures — it is an integrated approach to Multiple Intelligences. As in the area of cooperative learning, the Kagans are providing structures for Multiple Intelligences which teachers can learn today and apply tomorrow and for a lifetime.

The Kagan Structures are easy to learn and implement, fun for teachers and students, and produce profoundly positive outcomes along a remarkable number of dimensions. Different structures are designed for different outcomes, including enhanced mastery of subject matter, improved thinking skills, teambuilding, classbuilding, development of social character and social skills, communication skills, classroom management, classroom discipline, and development and engagement of each of the Multiple Intelligences.

The demand for training of teachers and training of trainers in Kagan Structures has led the Kagans to form one of the world's foremost training companies for teachers. Dr. Kagan's wife, Laurie Kagan, former Director of Elementary Education for the state of Nevada, directs all workshop design, development of training materials, and training of trainers. She personally trains and selects all Kagan trainers who go through a highly effective training process designed to ensure clients will have the very highest quality training possible. At present there are approximately forty Kagan Certified Trainers across the United States and other countries, providing keynotes, awareness sessions, workshops, and multi-day institutes.

Kagan Professional Development conducts training institutes and seminars worldwide. Kagan Publishing is the world's largest publisher and distributor of cooperative learning and Multiple Intelligences books and resources.

The spirit of Kagan is evident at all levels of the company. Kagan employees — from shipping clerks, to workshop registrars, to national presenters — enjoy the reputation of being extremely teacher-friendly. The Kagan staff is dedicated to serving teachers and those who support them. It is our mission to improve education by providing the highest quality resources and trainings designed to create in teachers a love of teaching, and in students a love of learning. On a regular basis, attendees worldwide state that one of the Kagan institutes has provided their single most formative and enjoyable professional development experience.

structures for success!

workshop Agenda

- Housekeeping
- Overview
- Classbuilding
- Teambuilding
- Rationale
- Model Teacher ABC
- Kagan Structures vs. Group Work
- Testing PIES
- Forming Teams
- Review
- Wrap

Three Goals for This Workshop

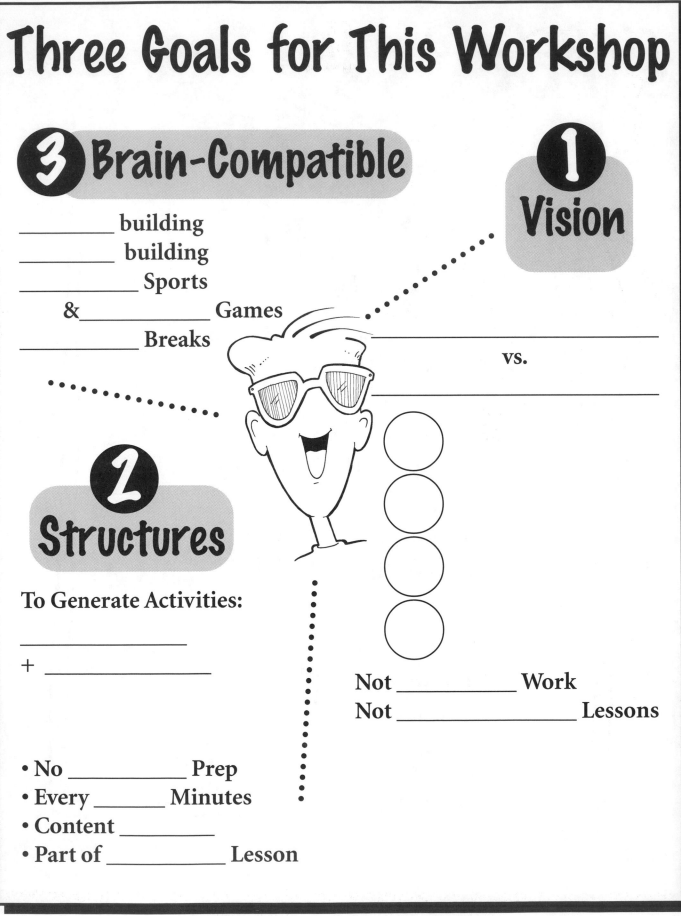

3 Brain-Compatible

_____ building
_____ building
_____ Sports
&_____ Games
_____ Breaks

1 Vision

_____
vs.
_____

2 Structures

To Generate Activities:

_____
+ _____

Not _____ Work
Not _____ Lessons

• No _____ Prep
• Every _____ Minutes
• Content _____
• Part of _____ Lesson

Hot Tips

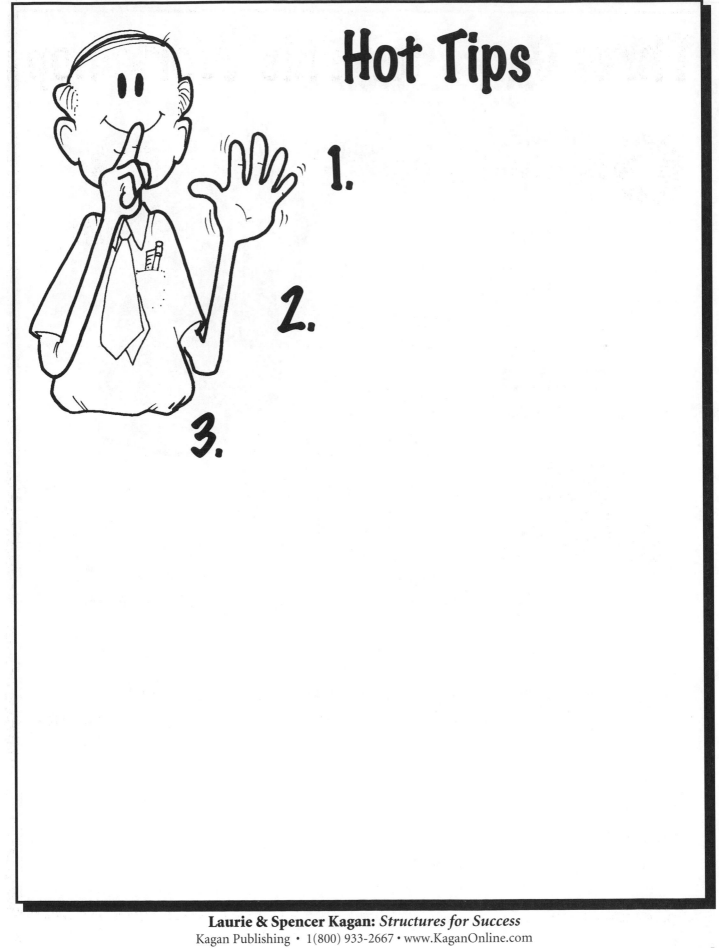

1.

2.

3.

Mix-Pair-Share

Students pair with classmates to discuss questions posed by the teacher.

STEPS

Setup: Teacher prepares discussion questions to ask students.

1 Students silently ___ around the room.

2 Teacher calls _____.

3 Students pair up with the person closest to them and do a high five. Students who haven't found a partner ____ their ____ to find each other.

4 Teacher asks a question and gives _____ ____.

5 Students share with their partners using:
- _____ _____ _____
- _____
- _____

Timed Pair Share

Partners take timed turns listening and sharing.

S T E P S

1 Teacher announces a topic and states how long each student will have to share.

2 Teacher provides think time.

3 In pairs, Partner A shares; Partner B listens.

4 Partner B responds.

5 Partners switch roles.

Optional: Before Step 4, the teacher may provide response gambits.
Copycat response gambits:
* *Thanks for sharing!*
* *You are interesting to listen to!*

Complete this sentence gambits:
* *One thing I learned listening to you was…*
* *I enjoyed listening to you because…*

RallyRobin

In pairs, students alternate generating oral responses.

STEPS

1 Teacher poses a problem to which there are multiple possible responses or solutions.

2 In pairs, students take turns stating responses or solutions.

RoundRobin

In teams, students take turns responding orally.

STEPS

1 Teacher assigns a topic or question with _____ possible answers.

2 In teams, students respond _____, each in turn taking about the same amount of time.

Classbuilding

The process by which a room full of individuals with different backgrounds and experiences become a caring community of active learners.

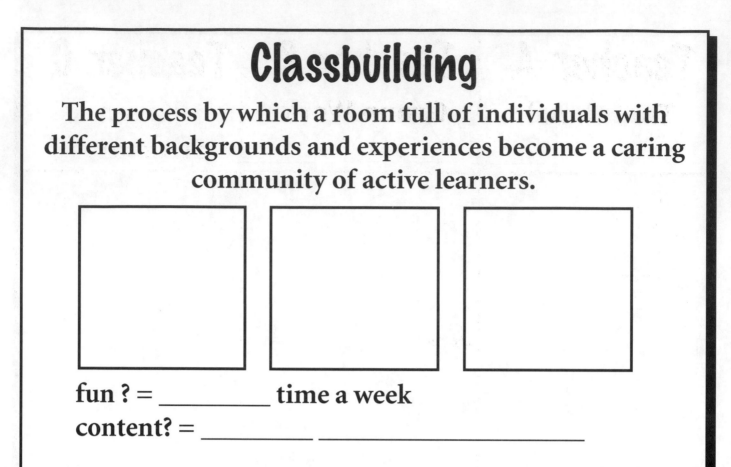

fun ? = _____ time a week

content? = _____ _____

Teambuilding

The process by which a group of four students with different backgrounds and experiences become a cooperative and caring team.

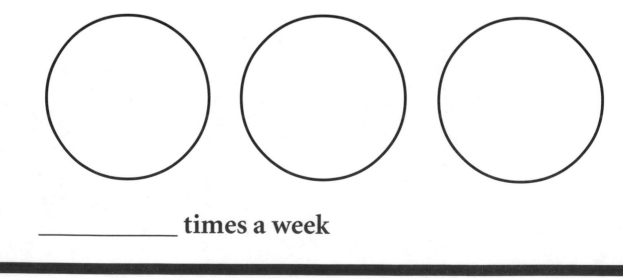

_____ times a week

Teacher A	Teacher B	Teacher C
Traditional	**Group Work**	**Kagan Structures**

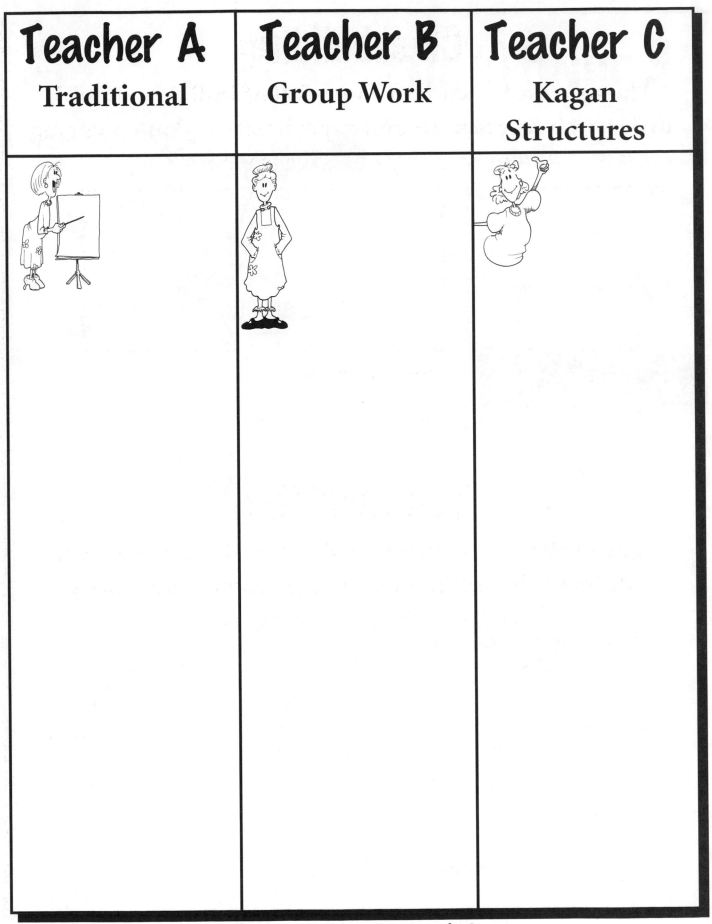

RoundTable

In teams, students take turns generating written responses, solving problems, or making a contribution to the team project.

STEPS

Setup: One piece of paper and one pencil per team.

1 Teacher provides a task to which there are multiple possible responses.

2 In teams, students take turns passing a paper and pencil or a pair project, each writing one answer or making a contribution.

Do the students in Teacher C's classroom get more?

Team Stand-N-Share

Teams stand to share their answers with the class.

STEPS

Setup: *Teams have a list of items to share.*

1 All students stand near their teammates.

2 Teacher calls on a standing student.

3 Selected student states one idea from the team list.

4 The student in each team holding their team list either adds the item to the list, or if it is already listed, checks it off.

5 Students pass their team lists one teammate clockwise.

6 Teams sit when all their items are shared. While seated they add each new item as it is stated, using RoundTable. When all teams are seated, Team Stand-N-Share is complete.

Stand Up, Hand Up, Pair Up

Students stand up, put their hands up, and quickly find a partner.

STEPS

1 Teacher says, "_____ up, _____ up, and _____ up!"

2 Students stand up and keep one _____ in the air until they find the _____ partner who's not a teammate.

3 Teacher asks a _____ or gives an assignment.

4 Teacher provides _____ _____.

5 _____ share using:
- Pair Discussion
- RallyRobin
- Timed Pair Share

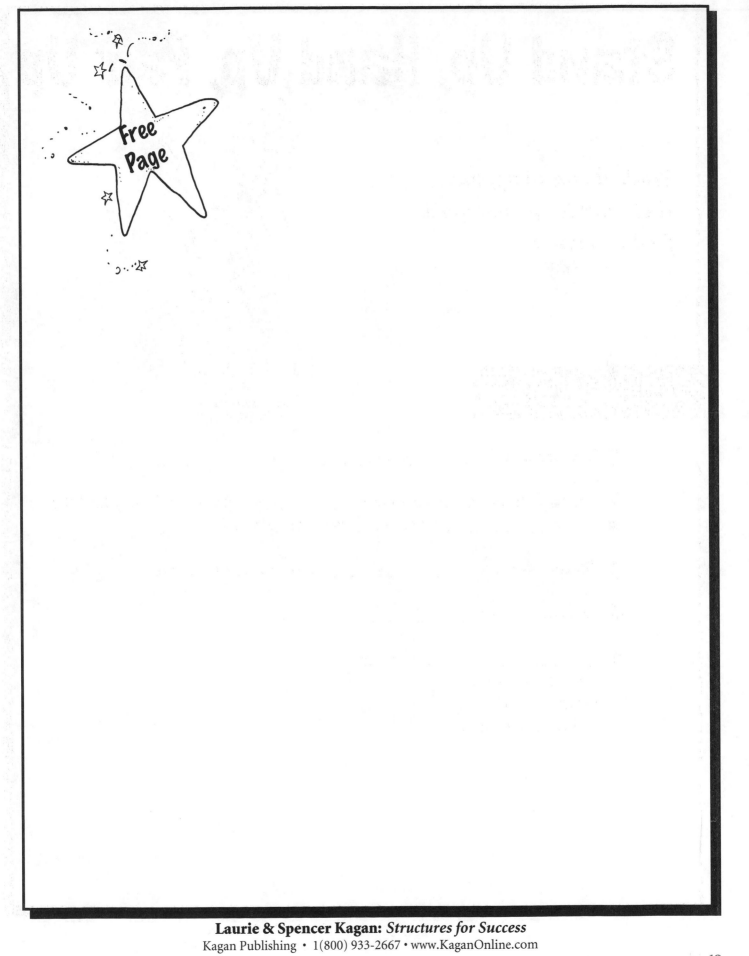

Free Page

Teacher A

Mental Math Addition

Complete each puzzle.

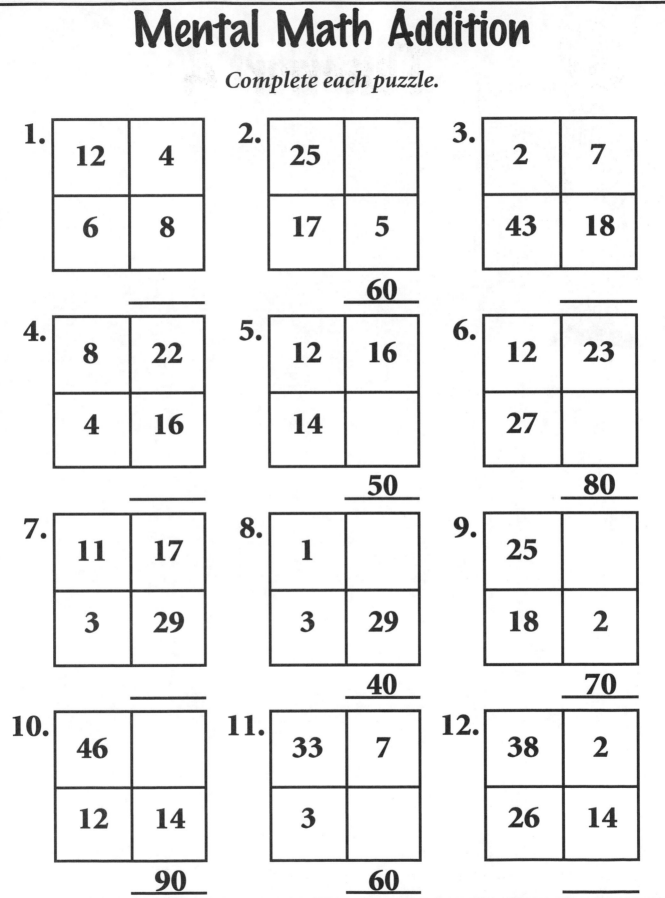

1.

12	4
6	8

2.

25	
17	5

_60_

3.

2	7
43	18

___

4.

8	22
4	16

___

5.

12	16
14	

_50_

6.

12	23
27	

_80_

7.

11	17
3	29

___

8.

1	
3	29

_40_

9.

25	
18	2

_70_

10.

46	
12	14

_90_

11.

33	7
3	

_60_

12.

38	2
26	14

___

Laurie & Spencer Kagan: *Structures for Success*
Kagan Publishing • 1(800) 933-2667 • www.KaganOnline.com

21

Teacher B

Mental Math Multiplication

Complete each puzzle.

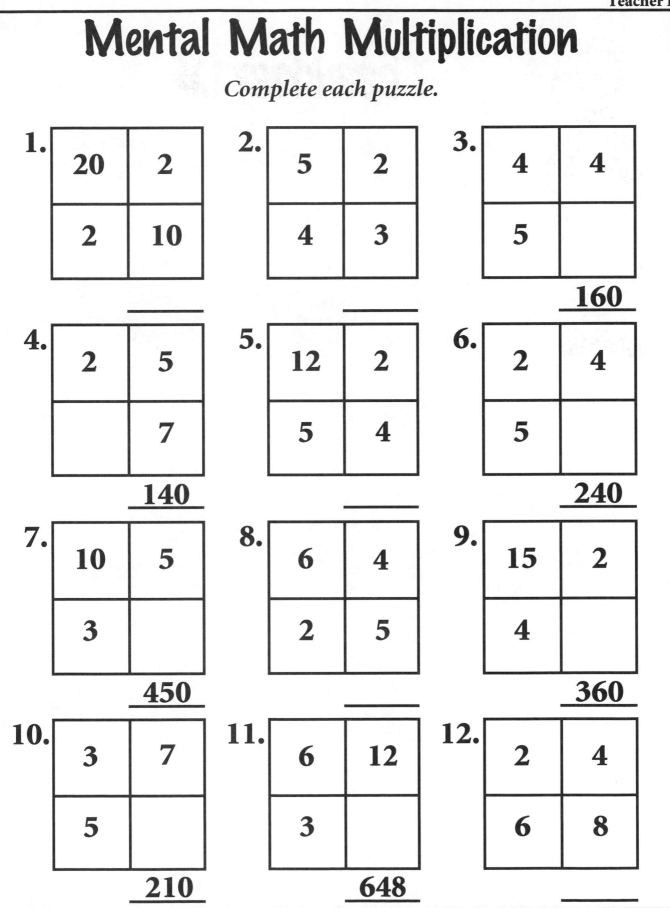

1.

20	2
2	10

2.

5	2
4	3

3.

4	4
5	

160

4.

2	5
	7

140

5.

12	2
5	4

6.

2	4
5	

240

7.

10	5
3	

450

8.

6	4
2	5

9.

15	2
4	

360

10.

3	7
5	

210

11.

6	12
3	

648

12.

2	4
6	8

Laurie & Spencer Kagan: *Structures for Success*
Kagan Publishing • 1(800) 933-2667 • www.KaganOnline.com

Teacher C

Laurie & Spencer Kagan: *Structures for Success*

Kagan Publishing • 1(800) 933-2667 • www.KaganOnline.com

Mental Math Squares

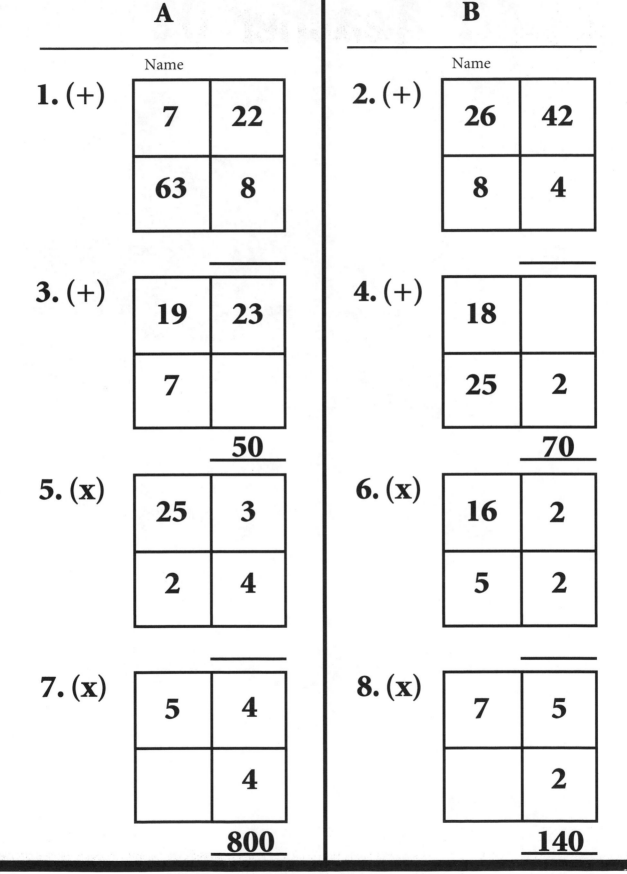

A

Name

1. (+)

7	22
63	8

3. (+)

19	23
7	

50

5. (x)

25	3
2	4

7. (x)

5	4
	4

800

B

Name

2. (+)

26	42
8	4

4. (+)

18	
25	2

70

6. (x)

16	2
5	2

8. (x)

7	5
	2

140

Laurie & Spencer Kagan: *Structures for Success*

Kagan Publishing • 1(800) 933-2667 • www.KaganOnline.com

Shoulder and Face Partners

Shoulder Partners
- High & Low Medium
- High Medium & Low

Face Partners
- High & High Medium
- Low Medium & Low

Laurie & Spencer Kagan: *Structures for Success*
Kagan Publishing • 1(800) 933-2667 • www.KaganOnline.com

RoundTable Variations

Laurie & Spencer Kagan: *Structures for Success*
Kagan Publishing • 1(800) 933-2667 • www.KaganOnline.com

RallyCoach

Partners take turns, one solving a problem while the other coaches.

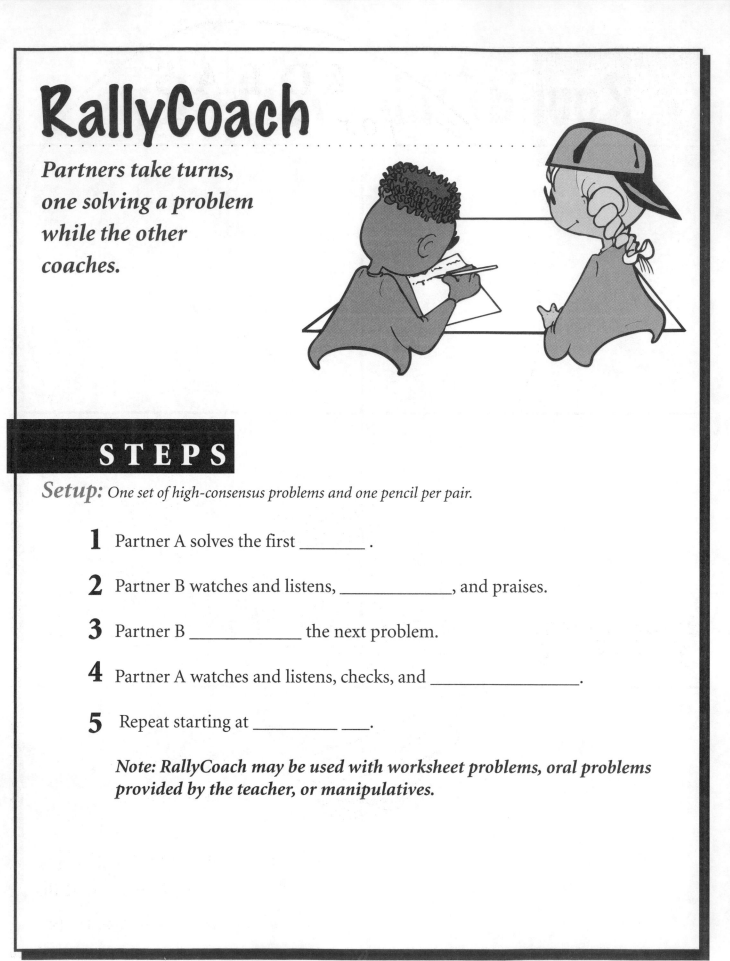

S T E P S

Setup: *One set of high-consensus problems and one pencil per pair.*

1 Partner A solves the first _____ .

2 Partner B watches and listens, _____, and praises.

3 Partner B _____ the next problem.

4 Partner A watches and listens, checks, and _____.

5 Repeat starting at _____ ____.

Note: RallyCoach may be used with worksheet problems, oral problems provided by the teacher, or manipulatives.

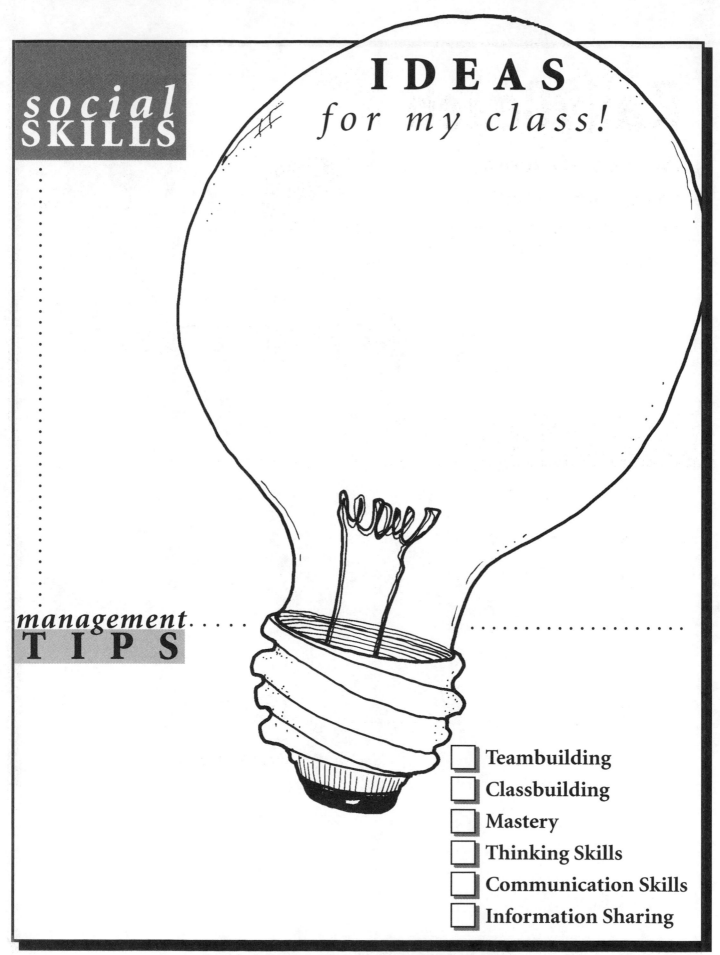

social **SKILLS**

IDEAS *for my class!*

management **TIPS**

☐ **Teambuilding**
☐ **Classbuilding**
☐ **Mastery**
☐ **Thinking Skills**
☐ **Communication Skills**
☐ **Information Sharing**

Laurie & Spencer Kagan: *Structures for Success*
Kagan Publishing • 1(800) 933-2667 • www.KaganOnline.com

Free Page

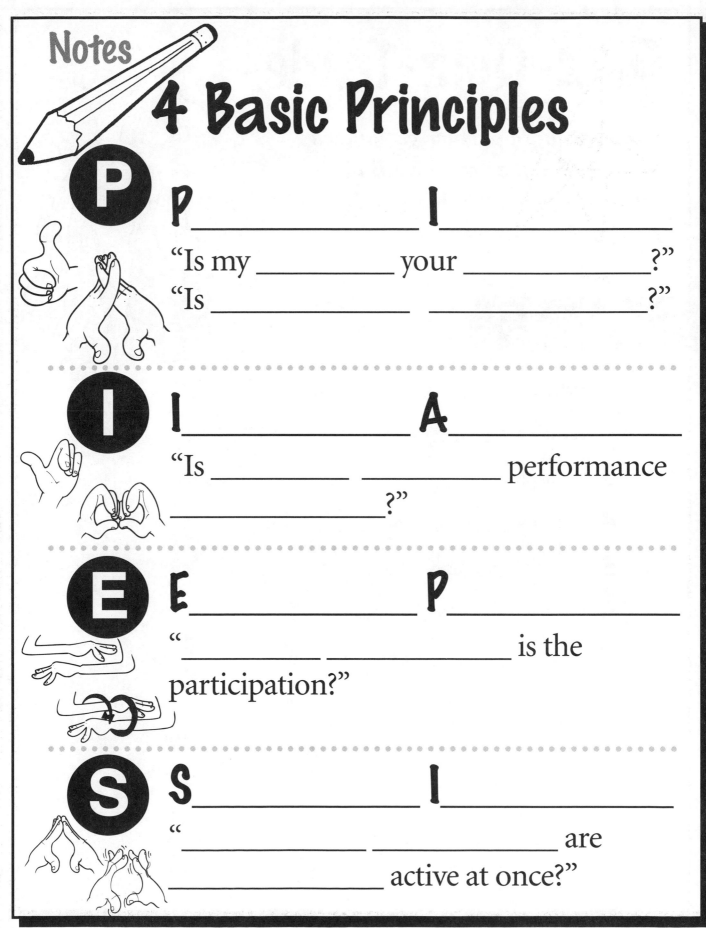

Notes

4 Basic Principles

P

P_____ I_____

"Is my _____ your _____?"

"Is _____ _____?"

I

I_____ A_____

"Is _____ _____ performance _____?"

E

E_____ P_____

"_____ _____ is the participation?"

S

S_____ I_____

"_____ _____ are active at once?"

Quiz-Quiz-Trade

Students quiz a partner, get quizzed by a partner, then trade cards to repeat the process with a new partner.

STEPS

1 Stand Up, _____ _____, Pair Up.

2 Partner A _____.

3 Partner B _____.

4 Partner A _____ or _____.

5 _____ roles.

6 Partners _____ cards.

7 _____ steps 1-6 a number of times.

Laurie & Spencer Kagan: *Structures for Success*
Kagan Publishing • 1(800) 933-2667 • www.KaganOnline.com

social SKILLS

IDEAS
for my class!

management **TIPS**

- ☐ **Teambuilding**
- ☐ **Classbuilding**
- ☐ **Mastery**
- ☐ **Thinking Skills**
- ☐ **Communication Skills**
- ☐ **Information Sharing**

Laurie & Spencer Kagan: *Structures for Success*
Kagan Publishing • 1(800) 933-2667 • www.KaganOnline.com

Forming Teams

Setup: _____

Step 1 _____ _____

Step 2 _____ _____

A. Math **B. Matrix** **C.** Remainders

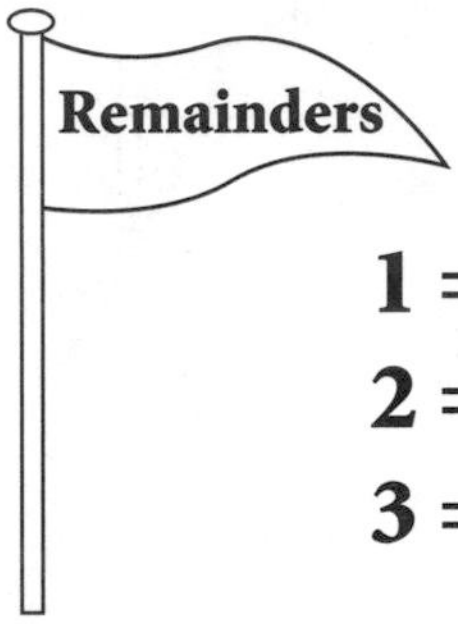

1 =
2 =
3 =

Step 3 _____ _____

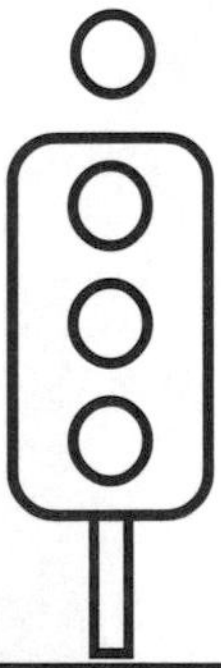

_____ = _____
_____ = _____
_____ = _____
_____ = _____

Tom

Step 4 _____ _____

Remember

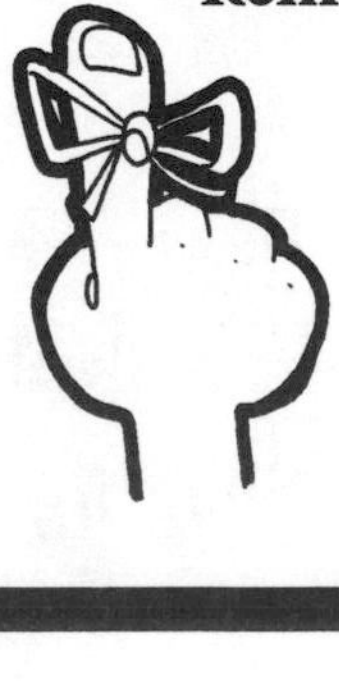

	1	2	3	4	5
B					
G					
Y					
R					

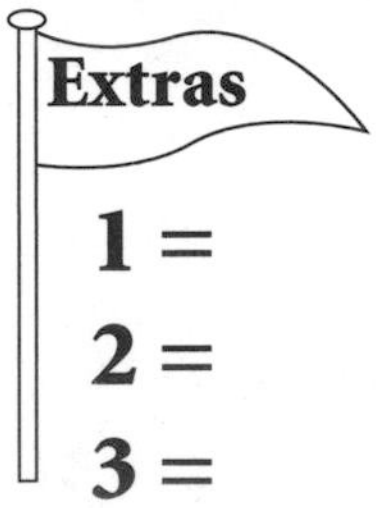

Extras

1 =
2 =
3 =

Six Key Concepts

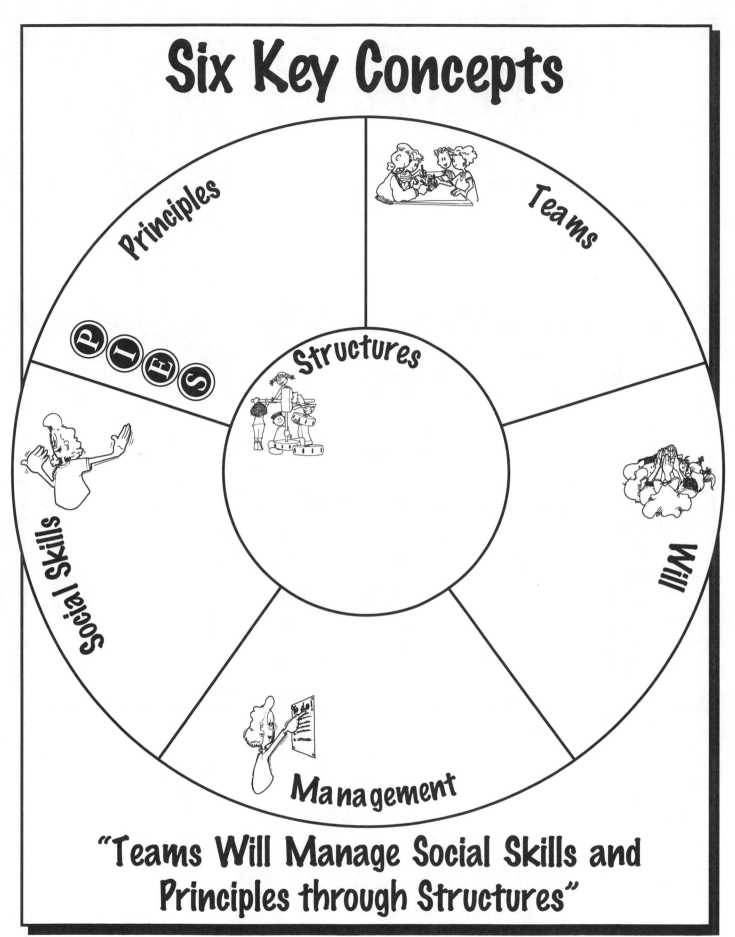

Principles

Teams

Structures

Will

Social Skills

Management

"Teams Will Manage Social Skills and Principles through Structures"

Reflections

Free Page

Free
Page

Free Page

Free
Page

Kagan Online Magazine

A FREE Quarterly Magazine on the Internet

Each quarter, Kagan Publishing & Professional Development posts a new Kagan Online Magazine on the Kagan website. You will find helpful teacher and trainer tips, step-by-step structures, downloadable activities, provocative articles, action research by Kagan practitioners, reviews of the latest Kagan products, professional development opportunities in your area, humorous education anecdotes and jokes, and hot links to other great teacher stuff on the Web. And did we mention it's FREE?

FEATURES:

- Teacher Tips
- Trainer Tips
- Structures
- Activities
- Articles
- Research
- New Products
- Workshops
- Anecdotes
- Hot Links

Visit
www.KaganOnline.com
for your
FREE Subscription!

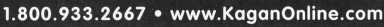

1.800.933.2667 • www.KaganOnline.com

Laurie & Spencer Kagan: *Structures for Success*
Kagan Publishing • 1(800) 933-2667 • www.KaganOnline.com

Host A Kagan Event

Kagan proudly offers a variety of professional development opportunities your school or district may host. Choose the best format for your teachers from a wide selection of exciting topics. Your teachers will receive world-class training at a site of your choice. Hosts must meet a minimum number of participants for the training, and provide the training location or help us find one. Hosts and facilitators earn money and/or vouchers toward the purchase of training materials.

Kagan Professional Development Events

Available as 1-day, 2-day, or week-long institutes.

▷ **Cooperative Learning**

▷ **Multiple Intelligences**

▷ **Win-Win Discipline**

▷ **Character Development & Emotional Intelligence**

▷ **Secondary Block**

▷ **New Teachers**

▷ **Training for Trainers**

How to Host A Kagan Event

1 Select the **Kagan Professional Development Event** of your choice

2 Call **Nancy Murray, Director of Workshops, Consulting & Graduate Programs**
1 (800) 451-8495

3 Enjoy your school or district's best-ever professional development event

Professional Development Opportunities

Cooperative Learning

Learn Kagan's easy cooperative structures. The focus of this in-service is instructional strategies to use as part of any lesson with little or no teacher preparation. You'll learn the basics of teamformation, teambuilding, classbuilding, management, scoring and recognition, assessment, the PIES principles, and a range of dynamic cooperative learning structures.

Multiple Intelligences

Teach to all eight intelligences, develop all intelligences, and create in every student an understanding and appreciation of their own unique pattern of intelligences as well as that of others. Learn simple structures which release the power of MI in any lesson.

Win-Win Discipline

Learn a host of strategies to use in the moment of a classroom disruption and what to do afterwards to prevent future classroom disruptions. Build student self-esteem, teach responsibility, and enhance engagement.

Emotional Intelligence

Boost your students' emotional intelligence. Deepen students' understanding of their own emotions. Learn and apply the Kagan Taxonomy of Emotions. Help students control their emotions and act rationally rather than impulsively. Encourage students to motivate themselves. Promote empathy. Develop students' social skills and character.

Character Development

Learn to promote the range of positive character traits through proven cooperative learning and social skill methods. Foster responsible and respectful behaviors as part of every lesson, with little or no special preparation.

To host any of these events, bring **Dr. Spencer Kagan, Laurie Kagan or a Nationally Certified Kagan trainer to your school, call Nancy Murray, Director of Workshops, Consulting & Graduate Programs**
1 (800) 451-8495

Block Scheduling and Secondary Restructuring

Leave this training ready to implement proven structures for today's secondary school students. Learn structures which create a total engagement for the entire block.

Hands-On Science

Teach science content and science process skills through easy-to-learn, easy-to-use hands-on cooperative learning structures.

Teambuilding and Classbuilding

Build caring and cooperative teams with teambuilding structures and activities. Your classroom becomes a caring community in which each student feels known, accepted, and appreciated.

Math with Manipulatives

Implement the best of NCTM standards, teaching every math concept at the concrete, connecting, and symbolic level. Teach for understanding through a range of powerful cooperative learning math structures.

Laurie & Spencer Kagan: *Structures for Success*
Kagan Publishing • 1(800) 933-2667 • www.KaganOnline.com

Kagan Professional Development Opportunities

Creating the Cooperative School

Administrators and lead teachers learn proven methods to bring staff, students, and administrators together to create the cooperative school.

Higher-Level Thinking Strategies and Manipulatives

Stimulate higher-level thinking through simple cooperative question prompts used across the range of curriculum areas. Learn to use the Question Spinners and Matrix, Spin-N-Think, Story Switchers, Higher-Level Thinking Question Cards, and the Idea Spinner. Your classroom becomes a think tank with cooperative learning structures and manipulatives.

The Multicultural Classroom

Kagan instructional structures are the natural way to create a caring classroom that honors and celebrates diversity. Learn research-based methods which improve race relations and create a cooperative classroom community.

Peer Coaching for Teachers

The best predictor of sustained implementation of educational innovations is peer coaching. Peer coaching enables change while holding teachers accountable for implementation. Learn models of peer coaching which provide the necessary pressure and support for change.

Cooperative Learning in the Primary Classroom

Primary teachers love our "lessons for little ones." Learn how to promote social and academic gains through proven structures for primary students.

Second Language Learning through Cooperative Learning

Your second-language learners acquire English or any other second language with ease through dozens of cooperative and communicative structures. Designed for ESL and foreign language teachers.

Social Studies

Teach to the themes recommended by the National Council of Social Studies through proven cooperative learning and Multiple Intelligences methods. Students learn the fundamental principles of democracy, through cooperative, democratic classroom structures.

Creating the Inclusive Classroom

Kagan's cooperative structures create an inclusive, cooperative community for all students. Learn special adaptations for the range of special need students.

Kagan

structures for
success!

Laurie & Spencer Kagan: *Structures for Success*

Kagan Publishing • 1(800) 933-2667 • www.KaganOnline.com

Cooperative Learning

Dr. Spencer Kagan (All Grades)

Practical and easy-to-use, this classic (over one quarter of a million copies in print) has been acclaimed as the single most comprehensive book on cooperative learning. This is the book which is leading teachers world wide to transform their lessons—to make cooperative learning part of every lesson! Have you heard about Numbered Heads Together, Pairs Compare, or Co-op Co-op? Learn about them from the man who created most co-op "structures." Would you like dozens of down-to-earth management tips? How about improving your students' social skills? Or 100's of ready-to-use teambuilding and classbuilding activities to make your class click? This book has it all. You will find easy, step-by-step approaches to teamformation, classroom set-up and management, thinking skills and mastery, lesson planning, scoring and recognition, and research and theory. Tables, graphics and reproducibles make cooperative learning easy, fun, and successful. 392 pages. **BCL**

Cooperative Learning SmartCard

Kagan's approach to cooperative learning is summarized on this colorful, laminated SmartCard. We highly recommend this handy little quick-reference card to anyone purchasing the book, Cooperative Learning. On the front of the card, you'll pick up tips on how to tighten up your cooperative learning lessons using PIES. On the center spread you'll find Kagan's 6 Key Concepts to successful cooperative learning. It includes the answers to the most frequently asked questions about using Kagan. On the back of the card, there's a list of Kagan Structures to assist you in lesson planning. Need a structure for introducing your lesson? Or how about one that engages the visual/spatial intelligence? Or want a teambuilding or classbuilding structure idea? Kagan Structures are categorized for you to make lesson planning a snap. **TKC**

Kagan Cooperative Learning Structures for Success SmartCard

Included in this tri-fold SmartCard are 28 of Kagan's very best cooperative learning structures. With these structures, you won't have to worry if you're cooperative learning lessons respect the principles known to increase student achievement and improve social relations. These simple, yet powerful structures always work because the basic principles are built in! The structures are easy-to-learn, easy-to-use, fun, and engaging. Students love them. Achievement increases. Let them work for you. **TSC**

To order:

1 (800) 933-2667 **www.KaganOnline.com**

Teambuilding

Laurie, Miguel & Spencer Kagan (All Grades)

When students have the desire and ability to work together as a team, something magical happens—**T**ogether **E**veryone **A**chieves **M**ore! Students like working together, academic achievement goes up, and discipline problems become a thing of the past. Includes step-by-step instructions, hints, variations, over 100 teambuilding activities and ready-to-use blackline masters for each of 14 favorite teambuilding structures like: Find-the-Fib, Team Interview, Same-Different. Promote a positive class and team atmosphere in your classroom and watch as your students work together in harmony. 178 pages. **BKT**

Classbuilding

Miguel Kagan, Laurie Robertson
& Spencer Kagan (All Grades)

Create a caring, cooperative class through energizing classbuilding activities! This best-seller includes step-by-step instructions, hints, variations, 100's of activities, and ready-to-use blackline masters for each of 11 favorite cooperative classbuilding structures like: Mix-N-Match, Stir-the-Class, and Who-Am-I. A must for the block schedule. Students are quickly and immediately energized—ready to tackle any curriculum. If you want to promote a positive class atmosphere with fun and easy activities, this is the source! 168 pages. **BKC**

SmartCards

Featured Products

TeachTimer

Just put the TeachTimer on the overhead projector and let it keep track of time for you! The TeachTimer counts either down or up, and sounds and flashes a "Time's Up" alarm. Great for giving students five minutes to write in their journals, two minutes for pairs to discuss a topic, or even 10-15 seconds of think time. Use the built-in chronograph to see how quickly students can line up, make a formation, quiet down, or solve a challenging problem. When it's not in use, the TeachTimer doubles as an overhead clock. A great management tool viewed anywhere in the class. Includes hard protective case and attachment to wear on neck for outdoor use. **WSTIME**

AnswerBoards Combo

8 Double-Sided, Write-On, Wipe-Off Dry Erase Boards;
8-Pack Color Markers; and 10 erasers

Increase engagement in your classroom. You ask your students a question. Is it better to have one student answer, or have all students answer? Great for everyday questions and answers. Perfect for Kagan Structures such as: Numbered Heads Together, Showdown, Find the Fiction, Pairs Compare, and many more. You'll make learning more fun while keeping all students actively involved. AnswerBoards measure 8.5" x 11" and are double-sided: lines on front for writing and a grid on the back for drawing or graphing. Try them. You and your students will love them. Set includes eight, long-lasting, easy-to-erase dry erase markers. They are fine point to make writing easier to read, and detailed work such as drawings, mind maps, and graphs, easier to create. **CWSAC**

To order: **1 (800) 933-2667** **Kagan** **www.KaganOnline.com**